Time. Less. Love.

Monika Singh

BookLeaf Publishing

India | USA | UK

Presentation by *BookLeaf Publishing*

Web: www.bookleafpub.com

E-mail: info@bookleafpub.com

ISBN: 9789363317857

First edition 2024

To the people who love deeply.

There is love for everyone; it will find you!

ACKNOWLEDGEMENT

My deepest gratitude to;
Universe for opportunity, courage and strength;
My daughter, for her existence in my life;
My husband, who made it all happen.

A special thanks to my parents and mother-in-law for being supportive in hours of need.

PREFACE

Have you ever fallen in love—once, many times, or with more than one person at once? Love transcends the boundaries of societal norms, carving out its own sense of right and wrong. Falling in love is effortless, but staying in love is the true challenge. The hardest part is enduring the painful transformation that ultimately manifests into a love that lasts forever. That's the essence of soul connections.

This poetry book explores the journey of two souls whose eternal love transforms into something timeless. Along their path, they face betrayal, mistrust, and deep misunderstandings, testing the very core of their bond. Their love undergoes a trial by fire, one that not everyone can survive. And yet, it is this very trial that makes their love unique—a connection that is not simply ordinary but eternal and transcendent.

Join me as we delve into this journey, where love begins with eternity and transforms into something enduring beyond time itself—*Time. Less. Love.*

Chapter 1: From the Memory Lane of Love Street!

Sparkles of New Love

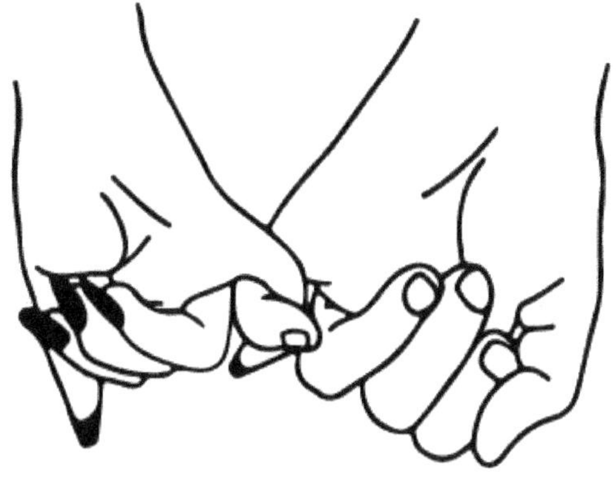

Like the morning light glitters,
Two hearts connect & spark flickers.
Eyes do the talking, while lips tremble,
Whisper promises; touch so gentle.

Hand in hand, spirits soar above,
Together, in this boundless love.
Vows & hopes interlace,
Two souls, perfectly embrace.

Blooming Love

In the mosaic of memories, where horizons
blend,
Lies a tale of love that will never end.
A tale woven in whispers of joy and grace,
In every memory, all I see is his loving face.

He came like a breeze on a summer's eve,
Cliche it may sound, even I couldn't believe.
I liked his attention & affection,
And looked forward to his appreciation.

No distance too far, no journey too grand,
He'd cross states for me, hand in hand.
He may not move mountains but travel roads
and trains,
Without caring, if it's winter, summer or rains.

Cuddled Hearts

In the quiet night, when the moon shines bright,
He watches me sleep, holding my dreams tight.
His gentle whispers, ease my fears,
In his embrace, vanish all my tears.

We watch movies but his eyes stick to me,
We cuddle like two lovebirds, one pod with two
peas.
His gaze, a story of love so deep,
In his arms, forever I'd sleep.

My legs stretch for the blanket's edge,
Yet I always miss, adding to my plight.
In one smooth motion, you cover me whole,
A comforting gesture that soothes my soul.

Rain, Romance and Aloo Chaat

Under stormy skies, our love takes flight,
Drenched in raindrops, together & alright.
In each other's arms, we laugh our worries away,
A dance in the rain, night turns to day.

As we promise, we'd brave any storm with
pride,
Be it stupid craving or together the world we
fight.
I'm craving for aloo chaat, and he doesn't care
for the pouring rain,
Hops on his bike, to ease my pain.

Bringing me aloo chaat, my craving to appease,
He's the only one who'd do this with such ease.
I am his queen, I accept with no shame,
Forever in my heart, written only his name.

With every raindrop and every kiss,
Of a love that's pure, an eternal bliss.
Hand in hand, enjoying our chat & aloo chaat,
Together forever, infectious love our hearts
caught.

Chapter 2: The Other Side of Love

Shadows Over Love

Then more happened to life,
They became husband and wife.
The bliss of love heightened,
Joyous moments are tightened.

Post petty fights, grudges hold tight,
Once fought with love, now ego is right.
Disagreement becomes conflict,
And true feelings restrict.

Loneliness in love

She sought time, claimed he was busy,
The silence grew, life's rhythm dizzy.
She weeps in front of him & in solitude,
He is unbothered, love seems rude.

She yearns for touch & love so pure,
He neglects her, that hurts much more.
It bothers her, so they drifted apart,
The pain she feels, in her heart.

Chapter 3: Smell the Freshly Brewed Betrayal

Hidden Secrets

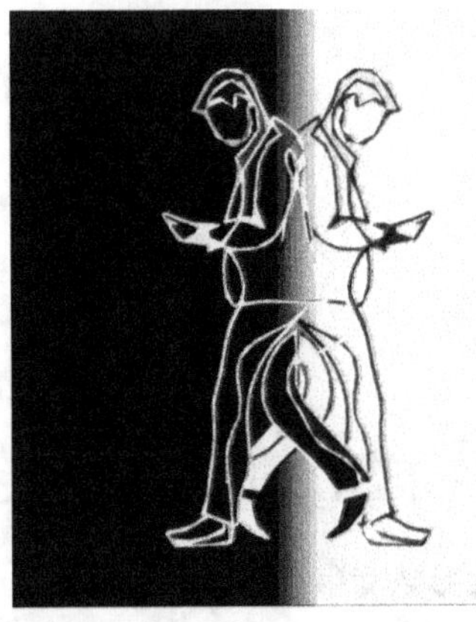

In your shining eyes, I saw my guiding stars,
And your touch, has always healed my scars.
Soaking high, believing love is pure and fair,
About to fall, unaware of the deceit lurking
there.

Your words, a melody full of lies,
My heart could not see my own plight.
Once my pride, my trust, my soul,
Foolish me, blinded in love, of the hidden hole.

Once a haven for my tears,
Your embrace took away all my fears.
But shadows whispered, laughing at me,
Revealing the betrayal cloak, I refused to see.

Betrayal's Sting

Betrayal's sting, a thousand bites,
Playing me like a puppet, in a web of lies.
No solace found, setting my dreams ablaze,
My love is betrayed, in a fiery haze.

Deceived and disgusted, I stand with no hope,
Burning into flames, a scared heart tried to cope.
A changed heart or my love, do you mock?
The illusion of perfect love bitterly broke.

A Painful Prayer

In silence, I feel the noise of chaos,
Wishing our paths had never chosen to cross.
My eyes cry & my heart aches,
Trusting you blindly, a harsh mistake.

Your lies, a knife cut deep right,
The pain, it echoes in day & the night.
Each tear, a testament to trust,
Broken by the weight of your lust.

My dreams are heavily blurry,
A timeless misery to carry.
A heart into pieces, no more love.
Yearning to release my broken soul.

Kill the Love, Long Live Ego

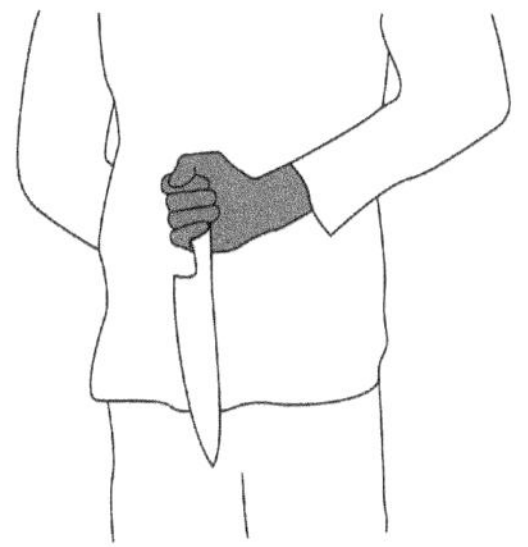

In the court of pride, our love was slain,
A silent crime, a gradual murder.
You danced to the music, without the rain,
Of unheard voices, echoing my pain.

A heart once full of love, now empty,
Sacrificed by the ego's dagger you carry.
You polished it well with the sweetest words,
Twisted it slowly, until it bled & blurred.

Wasn't your heart in pain?
Didn't your hands ever shake?
Haven't your eyes then bled?
Or did you relish watching me break?

Kill the love, long live ego,
Your triumph, regrets were zero.
The game of ego, king of strife,
In love's demise, the end of life.

Chapter 4: Towards Healing

Trust and Love

In the garden of love, the flower of trust
bloomed,
Betrayal seeped into the roots, and the garden
was doomed.
Your smile, your sweet words felt like a dream,
Yet in your eyes, deceit did gleam.

A broken will, a shattered soul,
Mending wounds, rebuilding it all.
One piece at a time,
Yet from the ruin, strength I find.

Acceptance, Forgiveness

In acceptance, peace I seek,
From my heart, you, I release.
All the stories & dreams are burned,
Betrayal's sting, a lesson learned.

The wounds are healing, the scars will fade,
You are now worthless, my heart will upgrade.
My love made you special when you were
nobody,
I love myself more, now my heart is in my
custody.

Yet hope remains, a light to guide,
In love's true form, I will confide.
I manifest the love I deserve,
I am worthy of the love I preserve.

Chapter 5: The Survivor's Anthem

For I am a Born Survivor

Sitting in the depth of my despair alone,
Betrayed by the one I once called my own.
A man who once was my lover, my friend,
Now a stranger, a traitor, a bitter end.

A man who once had my heart and my all,
In his embrace, I would gently fall.
It was only me, his eyes would see,
His love was boundless, wild and free.

There stands a stranger, bitter, cold and aloof,
Unhinged, unaffected, unmoved.
Watching me shatter as a million pieces fall,
A love once celebrated, now lost in the thrall.

But I will rise from the ashes,
Stronger and wiser.
I will heal, I will grow, I will move on,
For I am, a born survivor. We

A Letter to Self

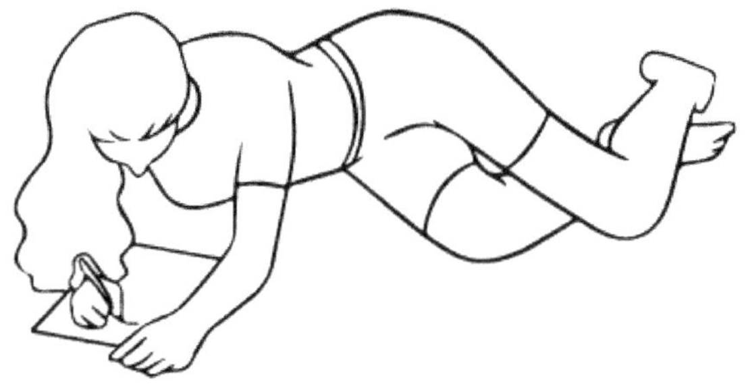

I hope you never lose yourself,
While loving someone else.
Giving giving giving, you may find,
It's a long way back to your heart & mind.

Love deeply, cherish it all,
A bad past experience, yet take the call.
Be ready to receive the love you deserve,
Understanding your worth, a learning curve.

You are your best lover & friend,
With you, the love will never end.
You will dance on your own track,
You will always have your own back.

Chapter 6: Renewals, Manifested Love

And We Meet Again

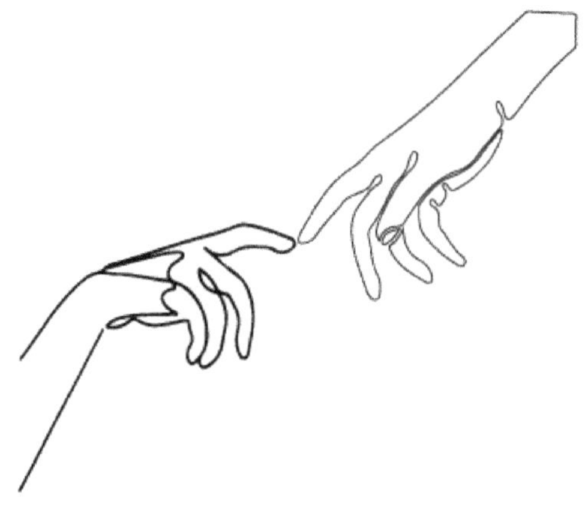

Ashes have gone cold,
Stories of both sides, told & untold.
Wounds are whole, gone is the pain,
Transformed by time, we meet again.

In the midst of ordinary days,
We reconnected in unexpected ways.
Eyes talking, words going beyond,
Heart remembered a timeless bond.

Pebble by Pebble

From the echoes of distant years,
Journey to transform & heal.
Two souls shedding fears,
Reuniting hearts to feel.

Pebble by pebble, brick by brick,
We rebuilt trust; it's love we pick.
The words are honest, ways are new,
A crimson love and a fresh drop of dew.

No shadows, no hint of grey,
The feeling never ends, together we pray.
Together we faced life's every turn,
In each other, our souls did yearn.

The Essence

On the slate of my heart, our timeless tale is
told,
A testament to love, in hues of black and gold.
Once celebrated each other as perfect lovers,
Till fate's cruel hand left us to suffer.

Through betrayals and the broken hearts tread,
Towards fate, twisted karmic threads.
The darkest hours my life could ever gain,
My broken heart bled silently in the pain.

To heal the wounds, our souls grew apart,
Twin flames, burning near and far.
Became each other's guiding stars,
Because the forever true soulmates we are.

Chapter 7: The Conclusion

Twin Flames: A Journey of Love

The first time I connected with you,
Your presence felt like déjà vu.
The feelings were new yet familiar,
Written in hues of gold, a tale to hear.

Two parts of a soul, identifying the same,
Attracted together by fate's game.
Passions ascended, emotions went high,
We loved & laughed, together we cried.

Bonded by love, so rare and pure,
Troubled by the world, we are each other's cure.
Finding solace in each other's embrace,
A mirror of myself, nothing I'll replace.

Rekindle

In life, trial by betrayal pulled us apart,
Distance deepened inside the heart.
The path is unclear, shadows darker,
Our path separates, realising our fear.

Yet, despite the pain, growth began silently,
Healing wounds, transforming us patiently.
Separated & lonely, still the bond remained,
Little do we know, twin flames' love can't be
contained.

Reunion

After the storm, the skies are clear,
I receive love, without any fear.
Our souls healed, our love soared,
Twin flames' love, forever restored.

Our souls are old, but this love is new.
'Grace me with love, please, will you'?
Healing our trauma and scars that surfaced,
It was all destined & fell right in place.

Our journey, a tale of love, healing & grace,
Two souls become one, forever interlaced.
Our love, in this lifetime and beyond,
Twin flames we are, with a timeless love bond.